21st Century
Junior Library

DISCOVER THE OVIRAPTOR

Jennifer Zeiger

Our Prehistoric World: Dinosaurs

Published in the United States of America by:

CHERRY LAKE PRESS
2395 South Huron Parkway, Suite 200, Ann Arbor, Michigan 48104
www.cherrylakepress.com

Content Adviser: Gregory M. Erickson, PhD, Dinosaur Paleontologist, Department of Biological
Science, Florida State University, Tallahassee, Florida

Reading Adviser: Marla Conn, ReadAbility, Inc.

Photo and Illustration Credits: Cover: © Daniel Eskridge/Shutterstock.com; page 7: © Danny Ye/
Shutterstock.com; page 10: © Noiel/Shutterstock.com; pages 11, 14: © National Geographic Image Collection/
Alamy; page 12: © Kitti Kahotong/Dreamstime.com; page 13: © SciePro/Shutterstock.com; pages 16, 17, 18:
© Stocktrek Images, Inc./Alamy; page 20: © Xavier Fores - Joana Roncero/Alamy; page 21: Tylwyth Eldar/
Wikimedia Commons (CC BY 4.0)

Cherry Lake Press is an imprint of Cherry Lake Publishing Group.

Library of Congress Cataloging-in-Publication Data has been filed and is available at catalog.loc.gov.

Cherry Lake Press would like to acknowledge the work of the Partnership for 21st Century Learning, a Network
of Battelle for Kids. Please visit http://www.battelleforkids.org/networks/p21 for more information.

Printed in the United States of America
Corporate Graphics

Note from publisher: Websites change regularly, and their future contents are outside of our control.
Supervise children when conducting any recommended online searches for extended learning opportunities.

CONTENTS

Chapter 1:
What Was *Oviraptor*?   4

Chapter 2:
What Did *Oviraptor* Look Like?   8

Chapter 3:
How Did *Oviraptor* Live?   15

Glossary   22
Find Out More   23
Index   24
About the Author   24

WHAT WAS OVIRAPTOR?

It is a hot, sunny day in the desert. A beaked dinosaur sits on top of a nest of eggs. Everything is quiet. Suddenly, the wind picks up. A wall of sand blows quickly toward the dinosaur. The mother dinosaur huddles over its eggs. Soon the dinosaur and its nest are buried.

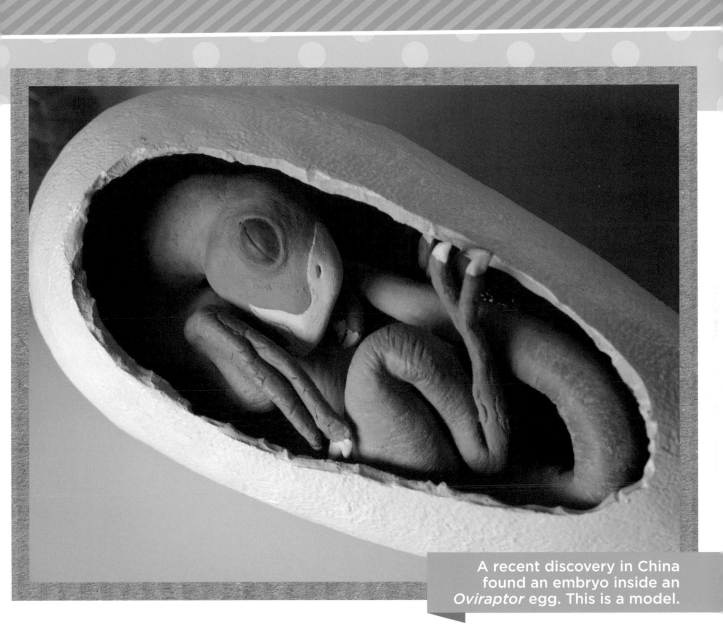

A recent discovery in China found an embryo inside an *Oviraptor* egg. This is a model.

This dinosaur is called *Oviraptor*. It lived about 75 million years ago. Its home was in a region now called Mongolia. Like all dinosaurs, *Oviraptor* is now **extinct**.

Scientists have found *Oviraptors* with eggs or near nests.

6

Ask Questions!

What was Earth like 75 million years ago? What plants and animals were around? Were they different from those you see today? Was the weather warmer? Colder? What other questions can you think of? Ask a parent, teacher, or librarian for help finding answers.

WHAT DID OVIRAPTOR LOOK LIKE?

Oviraptor walked on two legs. These legs were long and strong for running. The dinosaur's two arms were shorter and thin. Its hands could twist at the wrist. Three clawed fingers on each hand could grab and hold **prey**. *Oviraptor*'s long tail kept it **balanced** as it ran.

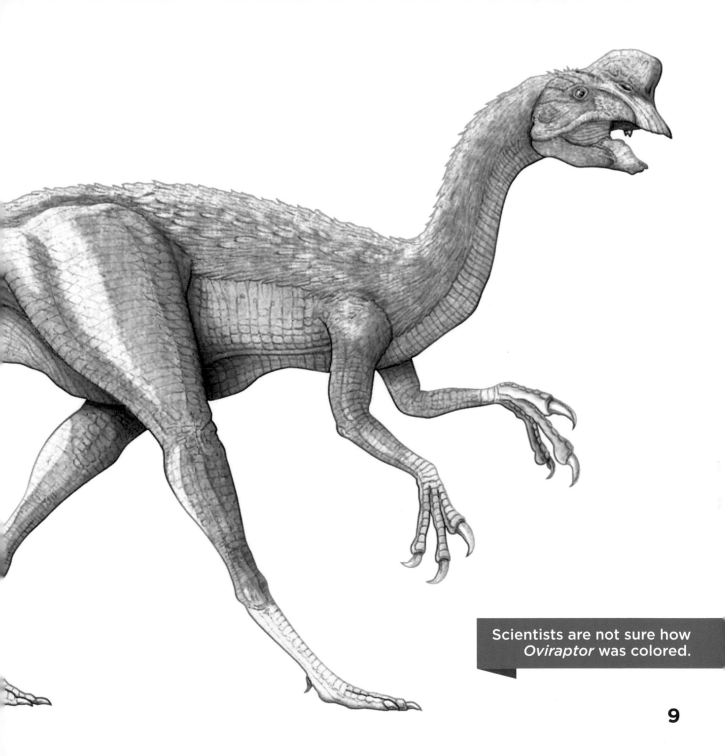

Scientists are not sure how *Oviraptor* was colored.

The dinosaur's head was oddly shaped. On top was a large, curved crest. Two large eyes were on either side of its head. *Oviraptor* did not have a mouth full of teeth. Instead, its mouth was a beak. The beak was sharp, pointed, and strong. It looked a lot like a parrot's beak. This dinosaur had a nasty bite!

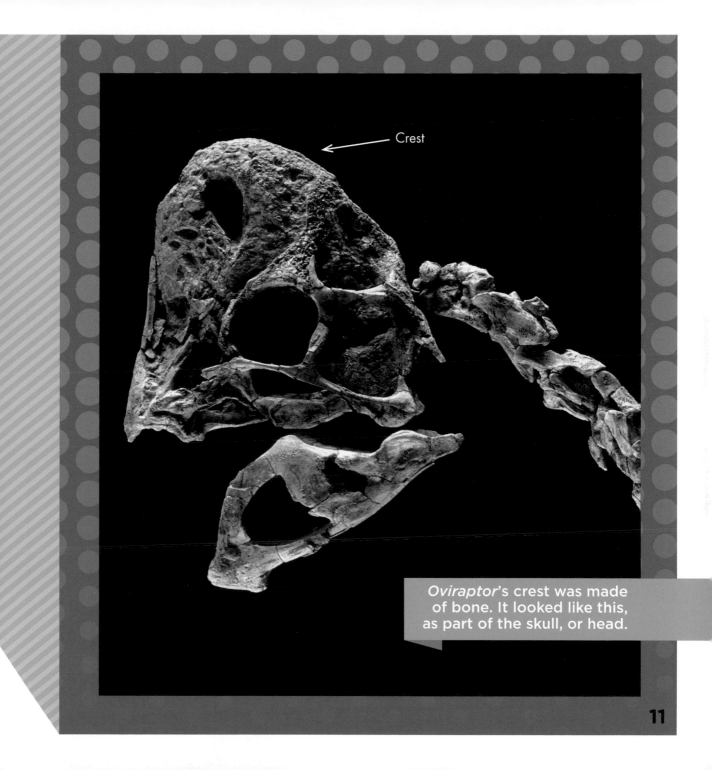

Crest

Oviraptor's crest was made of bone. It looked like this, as part of the skull, or head.

Oviraptor might have had feathers, much like modern birds.

Oviraptor was about as long as an adult human is tall. But the dinosaur was not heavy. It weighed around 60 pounds (27 kilograms). This is about the same weight as a golden retriever. Like a bird, *Oviraptor* had lightweight bones. This meant it could run fast without using much energy.

Look!

Scientists often compare dinosaurs to birds. Many scientists argue that dinosaurs are closely related to birds. Look at a picture of *Oviraptor*. How does the dinosaur look similar to a bird? How does it look different?

Oviraptor parents probably caught small animals to feed their young.

HOW DID OVIRAPTOR LIVE?

Oviraptor was a carnivore. This means that it ate meat. Experts think it ate mostly small animals, such as lizards. Lots of small mammals lived in the same area as *Oviraptor*. These probably made tasty snacks for *Oviraptor*, too.

Oviraptor used its good eyesight to spot prey. It quickly chased its prey down. The dinosaur probably caught and killed its prey with its claws. Then the dinosaur could take a bite with its sharp, powerful jaws.

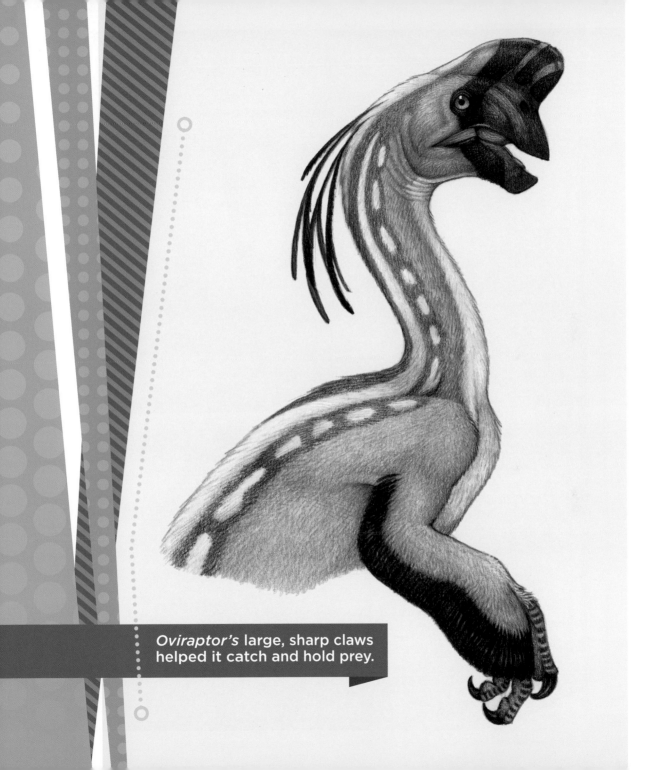

Oviraptor's large, sharp claws helped it catch and hold prey.

Scientists have found whole nests of *Oviraptor* eggs.

Dinosaurs laid eggs. *Oviraptor* cared for its eggs before they hatched. It might have sat on top of the eggs. This would keep them warm when the weather was cold. *Oviraptor* had feathers. These would shade the eggs from the hot sun.

Scientists know about dinosaurs by looking at fossils. Adult *Oviraptor* fossils have been found with dinosaur eggs. At first, experts thought *Oviraptor* was stealing the eggs when it died. But scientists studying the fossils found this was incorrect. The eggs were *Oviraptor* eggs. The adult *Oviraptor* was protecting its own eggs!

Visitors can see *Oviraptor* fossils at museums around the world.